A GIFT OF LEAVES

Books by Ardith Hoff:

A Thimbleful
A Gift of Leaves
After All These Years

A GIFT OF LEAVES
POEMS BY ARDITH HOFF

iUniverse, Inc.
Bloomington, IN

A GIFT OF LEAVES
POEMS BY ARDITH HOFF

Copyright © 2012 by Ardith Hoff.

Front Cover: "Persimmon Leaf" Photograph by Dr. Tom G. Holst
Back Cover: "Scarlet Tanager" Photograph by Terry Sohl

Illustrations:
"Skin" Intaglio Print by Ardith Hoff
"Jungle Cactus" Photograph by Tom Holst
"Marigolds" Photograph by Ardith Hoff

All rights reserved. No part of this book may be used or reproduced by any means, graphic, electronic, or mechanical, including photocopying, recording, taping or by any information storage retrieval system without the written permission of the publisher except in the case of brief quotations embodied in critical articles and reviews.

iUniverse books may be ordered through booksellers or by contacting:

iUniverse
1663 Liberty Drive
Bloomington, IN 47403
www.iuniverse.com
1-800-Authors (1-800-288-4677)

Because of the dynamic nature of the Internet, any web addresses or links contained in this book may have changed since publication and may no longer be valid. The views expressed in this work are solely those of the author and do not necessarily reflect the views of the publisher, and the publisher hereby disclaims any responsibility for them.

ISBN: 978-1-4759-2689-7 (sc)
ISBN: 978-1-4759-2690-3 (ebk)

Library of Congress Control Number: 2012908545

Printed in the United States of America

iUniverse rev. date: 05/23/2012

Contents

I.

Horses sleep	1
A Summer Hike	3
Wild Parts	4
Quatrefoil	5
Magic	6
Solitude	7
Song	8
Recomposure	9
Renewal	10
Iowa Summer	11
Dunning Springs	12
Skin	13
Scarlet Tanager	14
The Prophesy of Marigolds	15
Butterfly Flight	16
Music	17
On Turning	18
Monet's Lily Pond	19
The Floating Dream	20
Scarlet Tanager Returns	21
Leaving	22

II.

Clouds	23
Birds	25

Persimmon Leaf	26
The Language of Trees	27
Leaf Day	28
Gifts of Leaves	29
Meditation By A Brook	30
Hospitality	31
Melancholy Autumn	32

III.

Fourth Foggy Morning	33
How to Hear Snow Falling	35
The Sun in Winter	37
Winter Pantoum	38
Tulips	40
January Squall	41
Winter's Waltz	42

IV.

A Drizzle of Rain	43
Decorah Eagle Hatchlings	45
Spring	46
Mid-April Snow	47
Echo Valley Trout Stream	48
Unrooted	49
Cardinal	50
Willows	51
Final Thoughts	52

For my grandsons, Sean and Neil

1

Acknowledgments

Grateful acknowledgment is made to the editors and publishers of the books in which the following poems were first published:

"Leaf Day" in *Lyrical Iowa, 1983*; published by The Iowa Poetry Association, Affiliate of the Academy of American Poets, and the National Federation of State Poet Societies, Inc.; "Recomposure" in *World of Poetry Anthology, 1990*, published by World of Poetry Press. That poem was recognized with an Award of Merit.

I want to thank friends: Nancy Barry, Tom Holst, and Eugene Somdahl, for reading my manuscripts and making helpful suggestions. I also want to thank Tom for permission to use his photo of the persimmon leaf on the front cover, the photo of his jungle cactus blossom, and for his help in preparing the images for publication. I want to thank Terry Sohl for permission to use his photo of a scarlet tanager on the back cover.

I

Horses sleep
Standing in the shade
Neck over neck
While summer heat rolls by

A Summer Hike

A thousand tints and shades of green
In landscapes that shimmer with
Radiant heat against a cool cerulean sky,

A fragrant wind full of mountain columbine
Spilling into a shaft of light,
The taste of sun-warmed wild strawberries

And pennyroyal on the tongue,
A melodic murmur of water gliding over ledges,
Humming its thick, transparent tune while

Small marmots sit, alert, then scatter,
Darting behind cairns of stacked stones,
A flurry of tiny winged things rise

Into air, warm as breath, while birds ride
High on an updraft, banking into the breeze.
The whole world caught—suspended.

Wild Parts

Together we are more than
    the sum of many wild parts.

We are sun and rain and earth
    where many wild flowers bloom.

We are forests, streams, and hills
    where wild things tend their young.

We are oceans, stars, and windy plains
    where wild birds nest in shady quietude.

We are petals, branches, bright eyes, wings,
    and waterfalls, held together by gravity and grace.

Quatrefoil

Upon the gift of a four-leaf clover

A song
Suppressed
Is not music.

Joy
Cannot be
Suspended long.

Collect only
Smooth stones
For remembrance.

Cherish
Wild flowers
Where they grow.

MAGIC

With imperceptible sleight of hand,
Nature fashions first the leaf
And then an appropriate
Stem to hold it.

Not so with the jungle cactus,
There she seems to unleash her
Most-mischievous magic,
Having them bloom
With great abandon,
On wobbly stems,
Full tilt toward
Brazen beauty.

Solitude

A desert,
Quiet and dark,
Single phonotropic flower,
Needing words to bloom.

SONG

The notes between silences
    are lifting their slight weight
        on the tiny wings of wrens,

then, swooping down, they
    find small oval leaves
        with which to write

sonatas on the wind
    as light creeps across the sundial,
        the time for singing begins:

first the hoot owls,
    then the bull frogs, and
        finally, the soft violins

of crickets completing a harmony
    carried along by a stream, while
        eagles, riding the thermals,

perform graceful spirals
    far above the original notes,
        that keep on flowing along.

Recomposure

We are forests
Filled with light
And air,
Recording ourselves
In loops,
To be played back
Endlessly,
During darker hours.

Renewal

I can feel and
Smell
A change in the wind,

Rain
Will settle
The dust,

Damp clean Earth
Will swallow
From thirst,

And I
Will swallow
Refreshed.

Iowa Summer

How refreshing to return
After years in steamy cities
Among so many placeless people
Longing to regain lost dreams of Eden,

To live again on this peaceful patch-work
Of abundant earth, where corn and bean fields
Merge into a green-velvet, gold-fringed, tasseling
Topography.

Dunning Springs

I've traveled the world,
Seen many a falls,
Including
The great Niagara,

But my favorite falls,
And a peaceful place,
Are right up the road,
In Decorah—

The sound of water
Rushing over the rocks and
Burbling on down stream,
The songs of birds,

The buzz of bees,
The whisper of leaves—
I could stay all day
Just listening.

SKIN

Sitting in a blue-eyed tidal pool
Water whispering all around
Soft tongues lick my skin

Scarlet Tanager

(See back cover photo)

Sitting here surveying my orchard,
I see a quick flit among the grape leaves,
And watch your bright body rise from arbor
To tree top with such grace at landing, fragile
Twiglets barely quiver as you dip your bright head,

Feeling for the dark breasts of succulent fruit, your
Viripotent male instinct eagerly pierces the pink
Skin of cherries not yet ripe, yet sweet to your
Taste. Then, lifting your obsidian wings,
You rise swiftly and swoop away.

The Prophesy of Marigolds

On a melancholy morning
Burnt-Siena-amber blossoms
Answer my yearning for a warm surprise.

While mourning doves insist on sorrow,
Sun-bedazzled jewels tell no lies.
This day is meant for blooming!

Butterfly Flight

I rise
Through a halo of light
Gathering warm emotions

To wear as delicate wings,
And here in the dazzling air,
I ride the sultry thermals,

Then alight to find
A touch of tranquility
Among felicitous flowers.

Music

The music of your laughter echoes
>back to me,
In the ringing of raindrops on a
>metal roof,
In the west wind wafting
>through willows,
Mourning doves mating
>for life,
Their faint flute notes across
>a moist meadow,
A lone loon calling
>across the lake,
The sloosh, sloosh of your ores
>in the water,
Rowing that boat back to me.

On Turning

The sunflower fields are budding, and
At the exact moment of bloom,
They will turn their sweet faces

In search of the sun, just as
Newborns somehow know
To seek their mother's milk.

What is it that prompts us each in turn
To stretch forth again and again
Toward the sustenance we need most?

Monet's Lily Pond

Upon visiting Claude Monet's home at Giverny

They say that Claude had cataracts
When he stood beside this pond,
To paint his precious lily plants,
Short brush strokes in response.

They say the blues and purples went
As his sight began to fade.
The water seemed to yellow some
In the paintings that he made.

I've had and lost my cataracts.
To this I can attest,
Sky and water aren't as blue
Viewed through that muddiness.

But Claude, I think you did okay.
You painted what you knew,
Shattered sunlight on the water
Splintered shadows as they grew.

The Floating Dream

Rising above
Heavy summer heat,
I soar,
Then glide
On oceans of air,
Watching the clouds
Beneath me
Fold
In upon themselves,

Then part
To reveal
Sunlit fields,
And sparking water
Twinkled with stars,
And the breeze,
Ah the breeze,
Gliding me back
To my bed.

Scarlet Tanager Returns

After a long absence,
That beautiful black-winged
Red bird returns.
His splendid plumage
Stirring the stillness within me.

I want to enter his world.
I want to fly and feel the freedom.
I want one last chance
To forgo good judgment.

I want to enter that place where
Fantasy becomes a rational plan,
To feel, however briefly,
That pure pleasure,
Without longing or regret.

Though unwilling to relinquish the
Yearnings, I return to the conceivable
Knowing,
That circumstances more than choice
Will save me from myself.

Leaving

From the time the first yellow birch leaf flutters down,
    I can feel the summer leaving.

I can hear it start to crumble, like dry corn stalks
    entering the jaws of the combine.

Sudden access to pure awareness activates a pulsing
nerve in my brain—

So much to do and warm days waning, before
    summer thunder warns of autumn rains,

Frosty fields, and lopsided Vs of geese,
    struggling to align themselves for the hard flight into winter.

II

Clouds

One perfectly feathered cloud, pure white,
mimicking the outstretched wings of an eagle
below
persimmon-colored cumulus, bordered in purples.
A sumptuous sunset for a wonder-filled fall day.

Birds

A calligraphy of starlings
Sitting on a wire
Arise in unison
As though beckoned by bells
To some far-off home.

Persimmon Leaf

(See front cover)

The whole of the sun,
compressed in a single
luminous leaf—
gold blushing to crimson
along its vertical vein
tingeing its sinuous arching rim
red,

its heart-shaped form,
slightly furled
for maximum exposure,
equipped with vascular wings
for graceful transit through
trembling air,
brimming with fire.

The Language of Trees

In the inscrutable
Language of trees,
Their alphabetical leaves,
Bug-laced or
Bird-stained
Turn
Caution-amber,
Stop-red or
Stay green.

Gingko's sudden
Denudement,
Aspen's
Silver bottoms
Turned up by wind—
A portent of rain.

Don't you wonder
What other
Mystical messages
Are displayed
That only we
Wood nymphs
Can explain?

LEAF DAY

On this blue-gray morning,
A fleet of small birds
Sails across the field,
As though to make
Visible
A wind gust,
In the honest manner
Of landscapes,
Unafraid
Of their own true colors.

GIFTS OF LEAVES

I find them now and then,
Pressed between the pages
Of my favorite books, or inside
The envelopes in which they came,

Reminders that from time to time,
You thought of me, and sent these
Fragile messengers—
Each re-teaching me
What shared beauty is for.

Meditation By A Brook

We walk
in awe
across
a footbridge
over a
murmuring
stream
into
a cathedral
of trees,
a silent
confetti
of leaves
drifts
down
as we each
take our place
in this
most
sacred
space.

Hospitality

Autumn is an
unpredictable guest
who often arrives
on an inconvenient day,
packing frost and wind
and maybe even rain,
but etiquette dictates
that you be a gracious host,
that you compliment
the vibrant hues of her attire,
that you accept her apology
for arriving too soon,
that you invite her in
and build a welcoming fire
to warm her chilly toes,
and (in the process)
yours.

Melancholy Autumn

There is a certain longing,
    I'm not sure for what or whom,
      in the sights and smells
        of autumn,

In the dappled leaves of oak trees,
    with their subtle greens and golds
      and matchless
        deep maroons,

In the yellow light of morning
    and shades of purple in the dusk,
      that deepen
        way too soon,

In the smells of damp leaves burning
    and fresh-picked apples from the bin,
      their tart crunch bringing
        gooseflesh to the skin.

As the chilled winds start to fill
    the hollows of my heart,
      I feel shivers of delight
        and a little apprehension.

III

Fourth foggy morning
Trees full of filigree and flocking
Midwinter's frosty gift

How to Hear Snow Falling

From behind a window,
You can only see
But never hear
Snow falling.

You must go out in it,
Stand very still, and
Let the sound
Come to you.

You must listen
As though your life
Depends on it,
Holding

Your breath, and
Letting it out slowly,
Concentrating
On the silence.

It is then that
The brittle crinkle
Of flake falling on flake
Becomes audible.

This can be heard
Only by the most
Finely tuned ear,
With keenest

Imagination, and that
Perfect inner pitch,
Available only to
The profoundly deaf,

And the lucky few
Who take the time to hone it.

The Sun in Winter

There is a certain slant to the sun's rays in winter,
Not searing down as they do in the full burn of summer,
But silently shimmering across the sparkling snow,
The subtle illumination creating long shadows,
Even at noon.

Oh, how I envy that mysterious slant.
Oh, that I could learn such restraint.
Oh, to imitate that cosmic glow.
Oh, to be so serene and
Unafraid of the cold.

Winter Pantoum

The field is tinseled with snow
Red bird takes refuge from cold
Late-day shadows lengthen now
Fox circles pheasants in silence

Red bird takes refuge from cold
Thick cedars offer winter homes
Fox circles pheasants in silence
In search of a little nourishment

Thick cedars offer winter homes
Flickering wings flit in and out
In search of a little nourishment
The coldest of winter is upon us

Flickering wings flit in and out
A whitetail deer pauses to listen
The coldest of winter is upon us
Hoar frost comes drifting down

A whitetail deer pauses to listen
Crows announce a fresh roadkill
Hoar frost comes drifting down
Fox picks up on the clear signal

Crows announce a fresh roadkill
Just as a gibbous moon is rising
Fox picks up on the clear signal
The sun sinks below the woods

Just as a gibbous moon is rising
Late-day shadows lengthen now
The sun sinks below the woods
The field is tinseled with snow

TULIPS

Here in the dark of winter
Your bright offering of tulips,
Bringing back my belief in the
Beneficent world of springtime,

Luminous golds against green,
And that rare red line like a vein,
Leading to the interior of my vision,
Reality entered from a new direction,

Experiencing directly: the delicate,
Air between the touch and the petals,
Between the thought and the emotions,
Between the stimulus and the response

Of a spirit longing for wings, for
Tracing the feeling to an unknown
Region of the soul, where spring takes
Up permanent residence, once and for all.

January Squall

Snow, silently
   slanting down,
      sifted granules,
         finer than the finest
            white sand, forming
               wind-sculpted swells
             and breakers of snow
          on this in-land ocean
      called "Iowa".

WINTER'S WALTZ

One-two-three, two-two-three,
Cold-two-three, wind-two-three,
Rain-two-three, sleet-two-three,

Ice-two-three, snow-two-three,
Snow-two-three, ice-two-three,
Chills-two-three, chapped-two-three,

How long can this winter be?
Sun-two-three, rain-two-three,
Tornados and storms-two-three,

Leaf buds and wind-two-three,
Birds find their way-two-three,
Singing off key-two-three,

Will it be spring-two-three?
Sunlight stays longer now.
Birds sing much stronger now.

Winter stops waltzing now.
What a relief!

IV

A drizzle of rain
Spring's silver signature
In water and light

Decorah Eagle Hatchlings

A row of downy eaglets sleeping,
Budding wing over wing over wing.

Mother feeds them one, two, three,
Carefully coaxing open their beaks.

Big-bully brother demands the biggest bite.
Tiny newest hatchling just trying to survive.

Spring

Spring wafts in on whiffs of
lilacs, lilies of the valley, and
clover freshly cut.

Her clothing, quite becoming,
in finch gold, foliage green, and the
ruby of a humming bird's throat.

She strikes up a chorus of bird songs,
raindrops, crickets, and
baseball bats cracking.

She savors strawberries' sweet juices
and rhubarb's tartest bite, and washes
them down with dandelion wine.

She runs her fingers over stubbled soil,
and cradles downy ducklings.
Warm sun is her companion,

But beware! This beauty queen
dares to dance with danger:
lightning, tornados, fires, and floods.

Mid-April Snow

Daffodils, opening their mouths to rain,
Find their throats filled with lies—
A cruel fool's joke at best.

This chink in the smooth arc of spring
Has confused even thunder.
It rumbles with rage.

Mourning doves' coos have faded to silence,
But grackles punctuate the landscape,
Loudly scolding the wind.

Tire tracks, deep etched on the boulevard,
Have lost their way home.
The earth's warm lap has grown cold.

Here in my house, I sit wondering
When bright sunshine will usher in
Springtime gladness again.

Echo Valley Trout Stream

Rushing, gushing water
Rollicking over the rocks,
Slapping, slapping

Against limestone bluffs,
Shaping deep recesses
Where foot-long,

Freckled fellows
Lie lazily bobbling
Back and forth,

Wagging their heads
At the foolishness
Of fingerlings

Riding the rapids,
Toward
Unknown dangers.

Unrooted

Thoughts scatter
Like dandelion seeds,
Sent air born
By gentle puffs of breath,

And settle
On bleak terrain
Like a huddle
Of unrooted dreams.

CARDINAL

There he is,
A fatally crumpled
Cardinal

Dead
Among my flowers.

Was he absently
Admiring them
When he crashed

Into my window?
Or was he trying
To join me,

In search of
A poem
To explain
This perilous world?

Willows

Oh, to swing again
on the supple branches
of youth
in the woodland
wonders of
spring times past,

To bathe once more
in the wake
of swan's shallow
furrow,
rippled on
mirrored water,

our bare feet stirring
the alluvial sediments,
washing them
far down stream,
where new saplings
take root and grow—

oh, to swing again
on the supple branches
of youth . . . .

Final Thoughts

For my family and friends

While I am here,
I want to share
My life with you.

When I am gone,

I will be for you:
A blue heron
Rising out of the reeds,

A soft breeze,
Rippling
Across oat fields,

A silent snow,
Filling up
All your empty places,

A summer sun,
Like a warm hand
On your shoulder,

Letting you know,
I still love you.